SECOND EDITION

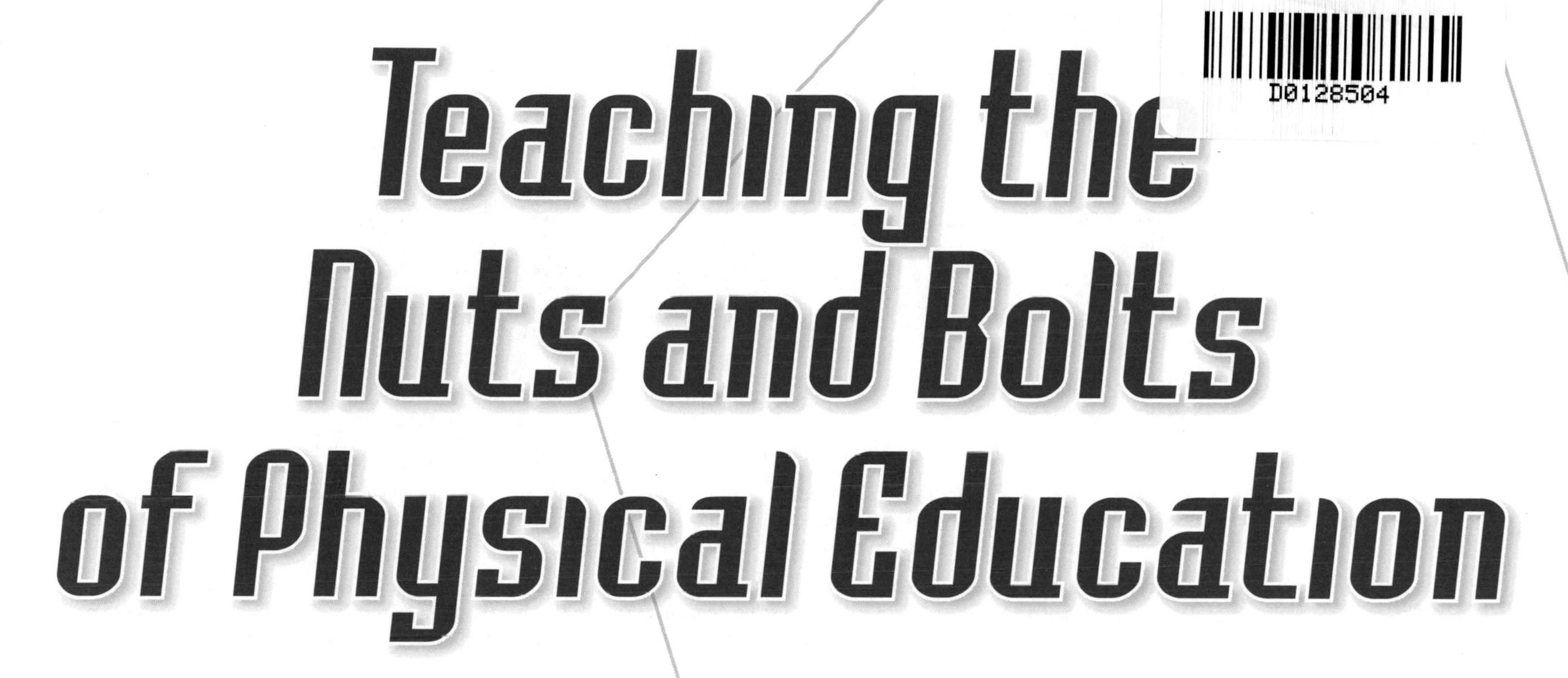

Teaching the Nuts and Bolts of Physical Education

AGES 5 TO 12

A. VONNIE COLVIN, EdD
Longwood University, Farmville, Virginia

NANCY J. EGNER MARKOS, MEd, CAPE
Broadus Wood Elementary School, Earlysville, Virginia

PAMELA J. WALKER, MEd
Red Hill Elementary School, North Garden, Virginia

Human Kinetics

Library of Congress Cataloging-in-Publication Data

Colvin, A. Vonnie, 1951-
Teaching the nuts and bolts of physical education : ages 5 to 12 / A. Vonnie Colvin, Nancy J. Egner Markos, Pamela J. Walker. -- 2nd ed.

p. cm.
Rev. ed. of: Teaching the nuts and bolts of physical education. c2000.
ISBN-13: 978-0-7360-6748-5 (soft cover)
ISBN-10: 0-7360-6748-5 (soft cover)
1. Physical education for children. 2. Movement education. I. Markos, Nancy J. Egner, 1949- II. Walker, Pamela J., 1953- III. Title.

GV443.C59 2008
372.86--dc22

2007025490

ISBN-10: 0-7360-6748-5
ISBN-13: 978-0-7360-6748-5

Acquisitions Editor: Bonnie Pettifor Vreeman; **Managing Editor:** Bethany J. Bentley; **Assistant Editor:** Anne Rumery; **Copyeditor:** Jan Feeney; **Proofreader:** Kathy Bennett; **Permission Manager:** Dalene Reeder; **Graphic Designer:** Robert Reuther; **Graphic Artists:** Yvonne Griffith and Angela K. Snyder; **Cover Designer:** Keith Blomberg; **Photograph (cover):** © Human Kinetics; **Art Manager:** Kelly Hendren; **Associate Art Manager:** Alan L. Wilborn; **Illustrators:** Roberto Sabas and Argosy; **Printer:** United Graphics

Printed in the United States of America 10 9 8 7 6

The paper in this book is certified under a sustainable forestry program.

Human Kinetics
Web site: www.HumanKinetics.com

United States: Human Kinetics
P.O. Box 5076
Champaign, IL 61825-5076
800-747-4457
e-mail: humank@hkusa.com

Canada: Human Kinetics
475 Devonshire Road, Unit 100
Windsor, ON N8Y 2L5
800-465-7301 (in Canada only)
e-mail: info@hkcanada.com

Europe: Human Kinetics
107 Bradford Road
Stanningley
Leeds LS28 6AT, United Kingdom
+44 (0)113 255 5665
e-mail: hk@hkeurope.com

Australia: Human Kinetics
57A Price Avenue
Lower Mitcham, South Australia 5062
08 8372 0999
e-mail: info@hkaustralia.com

New Zealand: Human Kinetics
P.O. Box 80
Torrens Park, South Australia 5062
0800 222 062
e-mail: info@hknewzealand.com

We dedicate this book to the many students we have been privileged to teach. Students of all ages have helped us become better teachers and enabled us to write this book.

Thank you.

CONTENTS

PREFACE

Teaching the Nuts and Bolts of Physical Education, Second Edition, is an innovative concept. Within this spiral-bound volume are the components for teaching locomotor and manipulative skills. Although each of the 8 locomotor and 17 manipulative skills span only two pages, these pages cover the essential elements for teaching and learning the skills. The first part of each skill contains the drawings, skill components, and cue sets for the skill. The next part describes the most common errors that occur and how to correct them. The last part provides a list of activities to reinforce the skill, including page references for the descriptions of these activities on the CD-ROM.

The simple yet thorough nature of this text is its strength. Drafts of this text were shared with college students studying elementary education. The students were enrolled in a three-credit physical education methods class that would assist them when they began their own teaching. Through the information presented in this book, students were able to break down skills, provide cue words, and correct other students' errors. The pedagogical improvement by students new to the field of physical education was amazing.

How to Use the CD-ROM

The CD-ROM contains everything that is included in the text and much more. When you use the book and CD-ROM together, you have access to everything you need to ensure that students master basic locomotor and manipulative skills. The CD-ROM includes the following features:

- Two types of assessment sheets for each skill. These partner assessment sheets break each skill into its component parts and include a brief explanation of the skill. We provide assessment sheets for children who can read and those who cannot. The CD-ROM format allows for easy photocopying.
- Additional activities to correct specific aspects of each of a skill's components.
- Many individual, partner, and group activities. These activities reinforce the entire skill, not just isolated components. When students have mastered a particular skill, the activities may be copied and distributed to classroom teachers to use during recess.
- Sample lesson plans. These scripted lesson plans are designed to be used when the skill is first introduced.

Enjoy this innovative text. The tools for teaching the nuts and bolts of physical education are all here.

Part I

LOCOMOTOR SKILLS

RUN

Eyes and Body

The eyes focus in the direction of travel, and the body moves in an upright position with a slight forward lean.

Flight

Both feet are temporarily off the ground in a stride position.

Arms

Arms are bent at about a 90-degree angle and move in a forward and backward direction without crossing the midline of the body.

Knees

Knee is bent to bring the heel up behind the body and parallel to the ground.

Cue Sets

- Eyes forward, pump your arms, big stride
- Arms bent, feet straight

Troubleshooting Chart

If you see	Then try this
No forward body lean	• Use a mirror or flashlight (reflection or shadow) to let the student see his body position. The student should have his side to the mirror or wall. • Videotape the student performing the skill. Using a remote to start/stop the action, show the student the tape.
No flight phase	• Encourage the student to run at a faster speed. • Place footprints or tape along a straight pathway approximately 40 feet long. The footprints or tape should be far enough apart to create a comfortable stride length for the student. As the student increases the stride length and speed of the run, periods of flight will result.
Arms crossing the midline of the body or not swinging with the run	• Have the student work with a partner. The partner must stand about 30 feet in front of the student. The student does a fast walk toward the partner, demonstrating the arm swing. The partner tells the student whether the arm swing is correct and lets the student know if the arms crossed the midline of the body. • Videotape the student performing the skill. Using a remote to start/stop the action, show the student the tape.
Foot not coming up behind the body	• Have the student run in place and try to kick her heel up near her body. • Have the student work with a partner. The partner watches the student run 30 feet and counts the number of times the student's foot does not come up near her bottom. The object is to score a zero.

Using Movement Concepts to Reinforce the Run

Have the student do the following:

- Run in general space while keeping personal space (location).
- Run in a straight line, a zigzag line, a curvy line (pathways).
- Run with a light force, a medium force (force).
- Run at a medium level, a high level (level).
- Run at a medium speed, run at a fast speed (tempo).
- Run forward (direction).
- Run with a partner and follow, lead, mirror (relationships).

Try combinations of concepts:

- Run in a straight line while following a partner
- Run in a zigzag pathway with medium speed.
- Run with medium force at a high level.
- Run at a fast speed in a straight line.
- Run in a straight line with fast speed and at a medium level.
- Run in a curvy pathway with medium speed while mirroring a partner.

HOP

Eyes and Body

The eyes look forward in the direction of travel and the body moves in an upright position.

Foot and Takeoff Leg

Take off and land on the same foot, bending the knee on landing.

Swing Knee

The swing knee is bent and swings forward.

Arms

The elbows are bent, and the arm opposite the swing leg moves forward.

Glide

The body moves with a smooth, rhythmic motion.

Albemarle County Physical Education Curriculum Revision Committee, 1996, 2-1.

Cue Sets

- Spring, swing
- Up, down
- Step and swing, step and swing

Troubleshooting Chart

If you see	Then try this
Hopping foot not coming up off the floor or landing knee not bending	• Using floor spots (or carpet squares if outside), have the student hop over the spots (squares). The student will need to bend the knee on the hopping leg to generate more force. • Videotape the student performing the skill. Using a remote to start/stop the action, show the student the tape.
Two feet touching the floor	• Use a wall or partner for support. • Using a scarf, pinny, or Dynaband, have the student hold the nonhopping foot up off the ground. The student tries to hop while holding the foot. The student can control when to put the nonhopping foot down.
Swing knee not moving	• Have the student stand stationary on one foot next to a wall. The hand opposite the hopping leg side holds the wall for balance. The student swings the swing knee while hopping in place.
Arms not swinging during the hop	• Once the student can successfully hop holding on to the wall, have him practice without the wall, swinging the arm in opposition to the legs.
Student not hopping with a smooth pattern	• Review the components of the skill. Being able to perform any locomotor skill smoothly requires the student to use the components of the skill correctly. • Select appropriate music or use a percussion instrument. Have the student hop to the beat of the music.

Using Movement Concepts to Reinforce the Hop

Have the student do the following:

- Hop in personal space; hop in general space (location).
- Hop in a straight line, a zigzag line, a curvy line (pathways).
- Hop with light force; hop with medium force (force).
- Hop at a medium level, a high level (level).
- Hop at a slow speed, a medium speed, a fast speed (tempo).
- Hop forward, backward, left, right, over, around (direction).
- Hop with a partner and follow, lead, mirror (relationships).

Try combinations of concepts:

- Hop in a straight line while following a partner.
- Hop in a zigzag pathway with slow speed.
- Hop with light force at a high level.
- Hop at a fast speed in a straight line.
- Hop in a straight line with fast speed and at a medium level.
- Hop in a curvy pathway with medium speed while mirroring a partner.

VERTICAL JUMP

Knees and Arms

Knees are bent and arms are back to begin the jump.

Feet

Feet are shoulder-width apart.

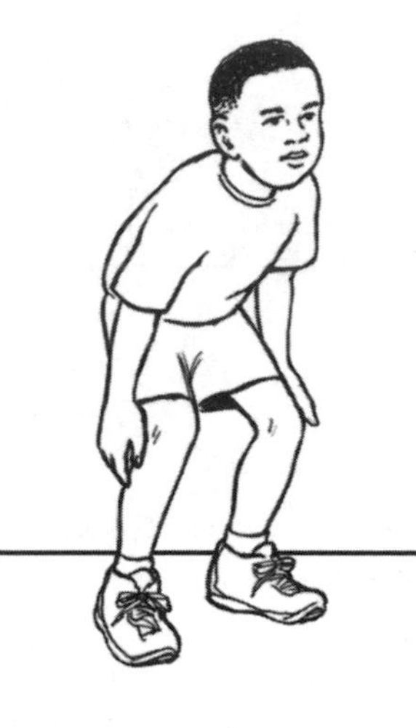

Arms

Arms begin to swing forward and up toward the sky.

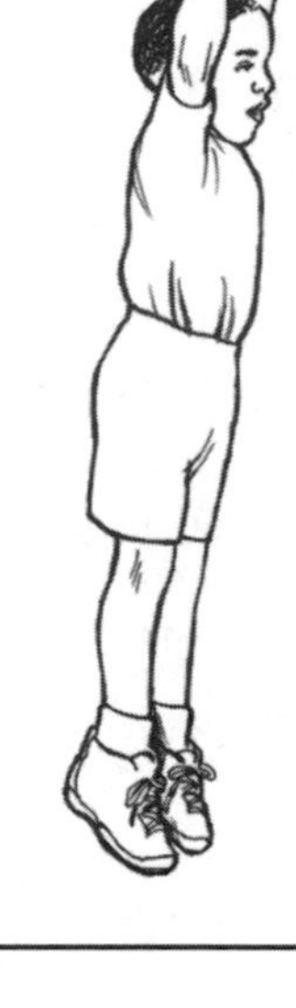

Legs

Legs forcefully thrust the body upward.

Landing

Knees are bent and shoulder-width apart.

Albemarle County Physical Education Curriculum Revision Committee, 1996, 1-1.

Cue Sets

- Swing, explode
- Swing high, touch the sky

Troubleshooting Chart

If you see	Then try this
Poor body position such as: • Knees not bent • Arms not back • Feet not shoulder-width apart • Body upright	• Use a mirror (reflection) or flashlight (shadow) to show the student her body position. The student should have her side to the mirror or wall. • Videotape the student performing the skill. Using a remote to start/stop the action, show the student the tape.
Arms not swinging	• Have the student practice swinging the arms and bringing the body upward so the weight shifts to the toes. • Suspend a rope between two game standards. Hang objects (aluminum pie plates, wind chimes, Wiffle balls) from the rope so the student can touch them if he stands on his toes. The student must swing the arms upward to try to touch the objects while bringing the body weight up onto the toes.
Student not forcefully pushing with legs and extending the body upward during flight	• Attach a sheet of paper to the wall. Have the student stand with his side to the wall, holding a piece of chalk in the hand closer to the wall. The student must jump and make a mark on the paper with the chalk. • Suspend a rope between two game standards. Hang objects (aluminum pie plates, wind chimes, Wiffle balls) from the rope so the student cannot touch them from a standing position. The student must swing the arms upward and jump to try to touch the objects.
Poor landing position such as: • Legs straight • Feet together • Arms behind body	• Have the student start on her toes and do a half-squat while keeping the feet shoulder-width apart. • Use a mirror (reflection) or flashlight (shadow) to show the student her body position. The student should have her side to the mirror or wall. • Videotape the student performing the skill. Using a remote to start/stop the action, show the student the tape.

Using Movement Concepts to Reinforce the Vertical Jump

Have the student do the following:

- Jump in personal space (location).
- Jump with light force, with medium force (force).
- Jump at a medium level, a high level (level).
- Jump at a slow speed, a medium speed, a fast speed (tempo).
- Jump with a partner and mirror each other's actions (relationships).

Try combinations of concepts:

- Jump at a medium level and land with light force.
- Mirror a partner as you jump in personal space.
- Jump at a medium level and land with light force.
- Jump at a slow speed at a medium level.
- Jump at a medium speed at a high level and land with light force.
- Mirror a partner as you jump with medium force at a high level.

HORIZONTAL JUMP

Knees and Arms

Knees are bent and arms are back to begin the jump.

Feet and Body

Feet are shoulder-width apart with a slight forward lean of the body.

Arms

Arms begin to swing forward and up in the direction of travel.

Legs

Legs forcefully thrust the body forward in a stretched position.

Landing

Knees are bent, feet are shoulder-width apart, and arms are in front of the body for balance.

Albemarle County Physical Education Curriculum Revision Committee, 1996, 1-1.

Cue Sets

- Swing, explode
- Swing, up, out

Troubleshooting Chart

If you see	Then try this
Poor body position such as: • Knees not bent • Arms not back • Feet not shoulder-width apart • Body upright	• Use a mirror (reflection) or flashlight (shadow) to show the student her body position. The student should have her side to the mirror or wall. • Videotape the student performing the skill. Using a remote to start/stop the action, show the student the tape.
Arms not swinging	• Have the student practice swinging the arms and bringing the body forward so the weight shifts to the toes. • The student works with a partner. Have the partner stand about 18 to 24 inches in front of the student. The partner holds up an object (hoop, picture, pinny) for the student to touch. The partner should hold the object high enough so the student needs to reach out and up to touch it. The student must swing the arms forward while completing the jump.
Student not forcefully pushing with legs and extending the body during the flight	• Have the student practice jumping over a hoop. • The student works with a partner. Have the partner stand about three to four feet in front of the student (far enough in front so the partner is not touched). The partner holds up an object (hoop, picture, pinny) for the student to touch. The partner should hold the object high enough so the student needs to reach out and up to touch it. The student must swing the arms forward as she jumps and tries to touch, not grab, the object.
Poor landing such as: • Legs straight • Feet together • Arms behind or to side of body	• Have the student do a half-squat keeping the feet shoulder-width apart and arms extended out in front of the body. • Have the student touch his bottom to the edge of a chair and return to a standing position. Repeat this activity several times.

Using Movement Concepts to Reinforce the Horizontal Jump

Have the student do the following:

- Jump in personal space, in general space (location).
- Jump in a straight line, a zigzag line, a curvy line (pathways).
- Jump with light force, with medium force (force).
- Jump at a medium level, a high level (level).
- Jump at a slow speed, a medium speed, a fast speed (tempo).
- Jump forward, backward, over, around (direction).
- Jump with a partner and follow, lead, mirror (relationships).

Try combinations:

- Jump in a straight line while following a partner.
- Jump at a high level and land with light force.
- Jump in a straight line with fast speed and at a medium level.
- Jump in a curvy pathway with medium speed while mirroring a partner.

GALLOP

Eyes and Body

The eyes focus in the direction of travel, and the body moves in an upright position with a slight forward lean.

Flight

Step forward with the lead foot and the back foot closes. Both feet are temporarily off the ground.

Arms

Arms are bent and swinging forward and back.

Glide

The body moves with a smooth, rhythmic motion.

Cue Sets

- Eyes forward, pump your arms, big stride
- Arms bent, feet straight

Troubleshooting Chart

If you see	Then try this
No forward body lean	• Use a mirror or flashlight (reflection or shadow) to let the student see his body position. The student should have his side to the mirror or wall. • Videotape the student performing the skill. Using a remote to start/stop the action, show the student the tape.
Feet not coming up off the ground during the flight phase or the back foot passing the front foot	• Using floor spots (or carpet squares if outside), have the student gallop over the floor spot. This will encourage the student to take a longer forward stride while galloping. • Place spots or "landing pads" on the floor. The student must land on the spot with the lead foot and bring the back foot to the edge of the spot, not touching the spot. Space the spots far enough apart that the student must take a longer forward stride while galloping.
Arms straight or not swinging with the movement	• Have the student stand with his back to the wall about one inch away. The student bends the elbows and swings the arms with light force toward the wall so that only the elbows touch the wall. The arms will have some limited movement. • The student works with a partner. The partner stands in front of the student with the hands up at waist level, open palms facing the student. The student swings arms to touch the partner's palms with the fists or hands.
Student not galloping with a smooth pattern	• Review the components of the skill. Being able to perform any locomotor skill smoothly requires the student to use the components of the skill correctly. • Select appropriate music or use a percussion instrument. Music with horses galloping would work well. Have the student gallop to the beat of the music.

Using Movement Concepts to Reinforce the Gallop

Have the student do the following:

- Gallop in a straight line, a zigzag line, a curvy line (pathways).
- Gallop with light force, with medium force, with heavy force (force).
- Gallop at a medium level, a high level (level).
- Gallop at a slow speed, a medium speed, a fast speed (tempo).
- Gallop forward (direction).
- Gallop with a partner and follow, lead, mirror (relationships).

Try combinations of concepts:

- Gallop in a straight line while following a partner.
- Gallop in a zigzag pathway with slow speed.
- Gallop with light force at a high level.
- Gallop at a fast speed in a straight line.
- Gallop in a straight line with fast speed and at a medium level.
- Gallop in a curvy pathway with medium speed while mirroring a partner.

SLIDE

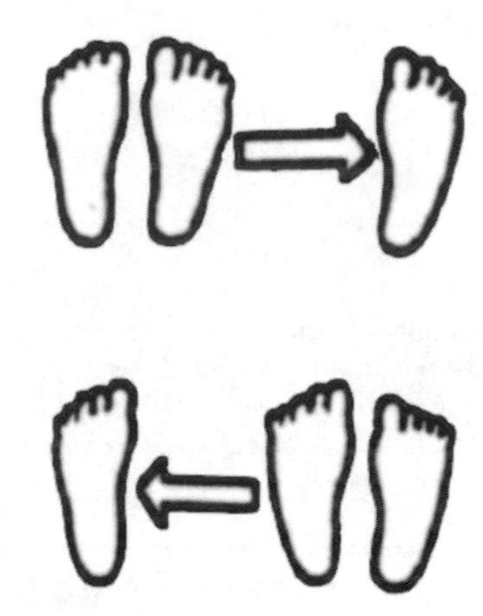

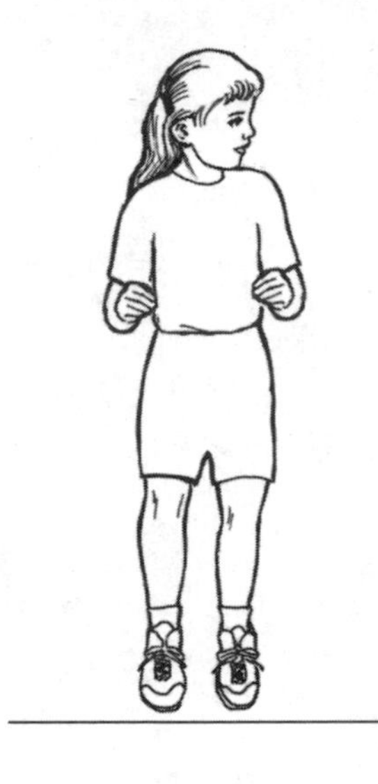

Chin, Eyes, and Body

The chin is placed over the lead shoulder, the eyes focus in the direction of travel, and the body maintains an upright position.

Feet

Feet stay parallel to each other throughout the entire movement as the body moves either to the right or to the left.

Flight

Both feet are temporarily off the ground.

Glide

The body moves with a smooth, rhythmic motion.

Cue Sets

- Chin over shoulder, feet parallel, move to the side
- Chin, step-together, step-together

Troubleshooting Chart

If you see	Then try this
Chin not near the lead shoulder or feet not parallel	• Use a mirror or flashlight (reflection or shadow) to let the student see her body position. The student should have her side to the mirror or wall. • Videotape the student performing the skill. Using a remote to start/stop the action, show the student the tape.
Feet not coming up off the ground during the flight phase	• Standing with his back to the wall, the student slides along the wall using a slow speed. Once he has the idea, he may increase the speed. • Using floor spots (or carpet squares if outside), have the student slide over the spot without touching it.
Body turned so the side is not leading the slide	• Standing with her back to the wall, the student slides along the wall using a slow speed. Once she has the idea, she may increase the speed. • Put a rope through a two-foot length of PVC pipe. Suspend the rope and pipe between two game standards. The student holds the pipe in both hands and slides along the length of the rope. Have the student repeat this activity several times.
Student crosses feet during the slide	• Standing with her back to the wall, the student places her hands on the wall. Using a slow speed, the student slides along the wall, maintaining contact with the wall. Once she has the idea, she may increase to a medium speed.
Student not sliding with a smooth pattern	• Review the components of the slide. Being able to perform any locomotor skill smoothly requires the student to use the components of the skill correctly. • Select appropriate music or use a percussion instrument. Have the student slide to the beat of the music.

Using Movement Concepts to Reinforce the Slide

Have the student do the following:

- Slide in a straight line, a zigzag line, a curvy line (pathways).
- Slide with light force, with medium force (force).
- Slide at a medium level, a high level (level).
- Slide at a slow speed, a medium speed, a fast speed (tempo).
- Slide left, right, around (direction).
- Slide with a partner and follow, lead, mirror (relationships).

Try combinations of concepts:

- Slide in a straight line while following a partner.
- Slide in a zigzag pathway with medium speed.
- Slide with light force at a medium level.
- Slide at a fast speed in a straight line.
- Slide in a straight line with fast speed and at a medium level.
- Slide in a curvy pathway with medium speed while mirroring a partner.

SKIP

Eyes and Body

The eyes focus in the direction of travel, and the body maintains an upright position.

Step and Hop

Step and hop on the same foot.

Arms

Arms move in opposition.

Flight

Both feet are temporarily off the ground. The nonsupport leg is bent as the hopping leg leaves the ground.

Glide

The body moves with a smooth, rhythmic motion.

Cue Sets

- Arms bent, step-hop, step-hop
- One and, two and, one and, two and

Troubleshooting Chart

If you see	Then try this
No step-hop or student using a gallop pattern	• Use colored floor tape to mark where the feet should be during the movement. Use a different color of tape for each foot. The same-color tape pieces should be approximately 5 inches apart, and the opposite-color tape marks should indicate a stride of about 12 inches. The student must step and hop on the first color and then switch to step and hop on the other color. • Videotape the student performing the skill. Using a remote to start/stop the action, show the student the tape.
Arms crossing the midline of the body or not swinging during the skip	• Have the student work with a partner. The partner watches the student skip 30 feet and counts the number of times the arms either cross the midline of the body or do not swing. The object is to score a zero. • Have the student perform a step-hop, pose. The student does the step and hop and then freezes with the arm opposite the swing leg forward and the arm opposite the hop leg back.
Foot not coming up off the ground	• Use several small rubber (nonskid) bugs for the student to hop on and squash. The student skips with one foot squashing the bug on the hop, then skips with the other foot squashing the next bug on the next hop. • Place 10 to 12 ropes in a line parallel to each other and about a foot apart on the floor. The student is perpendicular to the line of ropes. The student must step hop over each rope. Have the student do this several times to practice the skip.
Student not hopping with a smooth pattern	• Review the components of the skip. Being able to perform any locomotor skill smoothly requires the student to use the components of the skill correctly. • Select appropriate music or use a percussion instrument. Have the student skip to the beat of the music.

Using Movement Concepts to Reinforce the Skip

Have the student do the following:

- Skip in a straight line, a zigzag line, a curvy line (pathways).
- Skip with light force, with medium force (force).
- Skip at a medium level, a high level (level).
- Skip at a slow speed, a medium speed, a fast speed (tempo).
- Skip forward, backward, around (direction).
- Skip with a partner and follow, lead, mirror (relationships).

Try combinations of concepts:

- Skip in a straight line while following a partner.
- Skip in a zigzag pathway with medium speed.
- Skip with light force at a medium level.
- Skip in a straight line at fast speed.
- Skip in a straight line at fast speed and at a medium level.
- Skip in a curvy pathway with medium speed while mirroring a partner.

LEAP

Run

Take several running steps before starting to leap.

Takeoff

Push off the ground with one foot.

Flight

Both feet are temporarily off the ground in a stride position and the arm opposite the lead foot reaches forward.

Landing

Land on the opposite foot from the takeoff foot; knee is bent to absorb force.

Run

Run a few steps after landing.

Cue Sets

- Take off on one foot, get airborne, land on the other foot
- Run, fly, run again
- Go, push, fly, land

Troubleshooting Chart

If you see	Then try this
Student not getting the legs into a good stride position	• Have the student practice walking with very large steps. • Use a mirror or flashlight (reflection or shadow) to let the student see his body position. The student should have his side to the mirror or wall. • Place two ropes parallel in the play area and have the student walk over the ropes. Be sure that the ropes are placed a little wider than the widest stride of the student. This will provide an opportunity for the student to leap over the ropes.
Student using two feet to initiate the leap, or not getting enough height on the leap	• Videotape the student performing the skill. Using a remote to start/stop the action, show the student the tape. • Make a hurdle that the student can leap over: Using a pool noodle, one noodle connector, and an 18-inch cone, cut the noodle in half and put one half in each end of the connector. Then place the center hole of the connector over the top of the cone. The student will have to push off using one foot to do this activity.
Arms not involved in the action	• Find a picture of a hurdler. Show the student this picture and then ask her to try to look like the picture. You can use the pool noodle hurdles described previously. • Have the student practice walking with giant steps and swinging the stepping leg forward and up. The arm opposite the stepping leg should also swing forward so that the arm and leg are parallel.
Student landing on both feet	• Have the student run several steps, take a giant step while swinging the opposite arm forward, and begin to run again. Encourage the student to come up off the ground during the giant step. • Set up two ropes parallel to each other and approximately two feet apart. Place a landing spot on the far side of the ropes for the landing foot to touch.

Using Movement Concepts to Reinforce the Leap

Have the student begin with a run and then challenge him to do the following:

- Practice leaping in general space while maintaining personal space (location).
- Leap and land with light force (force).
- Leap at a low level, a medium level, a high level (level).
- Leap at a slow speed, a medium speed, a fast speed (tempo).
- Leap over, around an object (direction).
- Leap with a partner and mirror each other's actions (relationships).

Try combinations of concepts:

- Leap at a high level and land with light force.
- Mirror a partner as you leap in general space.
- Leap at a slow speed at a medium level.
- Leap at a medium speed at a high level and land with light force.
- Mirror a partner as you leap at a medium level and land with light force.

Part II

MANIPULATIVE SKILLS

UNDERHAND ROLL

Ready Position

Facing target, feet shoulder-width apart, knees bent, eyes on target, object held in dominant hand (palm up) in front of the body.

Arm Back

Swing the rolling arm back at least to waist level.

Step and Roll

Step forward with the opposite foot, swing the rolling arm forward, and release the ball on the ground (low level) while bending at the knees and waist. The front of the body should be facing the target.

Follow Through

Rolling hand continues toward the target in front of the body and finishes above the waist with palm facing upward.

Cue Sets

- Ready, arm back, step and roll, follow through
- Ready, arm back, step and roll, spider on the shoulder
- Ready, use your stepping foot, sneak up on the target

Troubleshooting Chart

If you see	Then try this
Eyes not on target	• Have the student roll at a target he has designed. • Use color targets on the floor and roll the ball across them. • Use pie plates for targets and place them on the wall at floor level. • Use targets the student must roll through (e.g., cones, chairs, horseshoes).
Arm not swinging back	• Have the student swing her arm back to touch a target (pie plate) attached to the wall. The target is placed at the student's waist level in line with the rolling arm. The student will then roll the ball. • With a partner standing behind the roller, the roller swings his arm back and tries to take an object out of the partner's hand. • Put butcher paper on the wall. The student stands sideways with a marker in her rolling hand. As the student moves the rolling hand back, she draws a curvy line on the paper.
Student not stepping in opposition	• Tie a pinny or scarf around the leg opposite the rolling hand. • Use spots or footprints on the floor to indicate the proper foot placement. • Tape bubble wrap to the floor. Have the student step in opposition on that spot to create a noise.
Hand not near the floor on release	• Place a toy truck on the floor where the hand should follow through and have the student push it forward. You could also try this with a tennis ball. • Have the student use a small whisk broom to sweep the ball forward.
Knees not bending to allow the hand to get close to the floor, or one knee touching the floor	• Slide a beanbag across the floor rather than a ball. • Take a flashlight or projector and shine the light on the student. Have the student watch his shadow as he performs the underhand roll. • Place a six-inch cone approximately one foot in front of the student's nonstepping leg. Have the student practice the skill without a ball and have him touch his knee to the cone.
Ball bouncing when released	• Have a partner check the hand position when the ball is released. • Stretch a rope between two chairs so the rope is approximately 12 inches off the floor. Have the student perform the underhand roll releasing the ball under the rope.
Student not stepping toward target	• Use a line on the floor or put down tape. Challenge the student to step on the line when the ball is released. • Tape bubble wrap to the floor. Have the student step on the wrap to create a noise. • Place two objects shoe-width apart in front of the student. The objects may be cones, domes, Styrofoam bricks, and so on. He must step so that his foot is placed between the two objects.
Body not in proper alignment on the follow-through	• Tell the student to point her belt buckle at the target on the follow-through. • Use a line on the floor or put down tape. Challenge the student to release the ball on the line and bring the rolling arm forward over the line when the ball is released.

Activities to Reinforce Underhand Roll

UNDERHAND THROW

Ready Position

Facing target, feet shoulder-width apart, knees bent, eyes on target, object held in dominant hand (palm up) in front of body.

Arm Back

Swing the throwing arm back to at least waist level.

Step and Throw

Step forward with the opposite foot, bring the throwing arm forward, and release the ball below the waist. The arm stays straight throughout the entire movement.

Follow Through

Throwing hand continues toward the target in front of the body with palm facing upward.

Cue Sets

- Ready, arm back, step and throw, follow through
- Arm back, step and throw
- Ready, arm back, use your stepping foot, let it go

Troubleshooting Chart

If you see	Then try this
Eyes not on target	• Have the student throw at a target he has designed. • Attach a color target to the wall. • Use pie plates for targets and place them on the wall at a medium level. • As an outside activity, have the student throw wet sponges at a target in an effort to soak the target with water.
Arm not swinging back	• Have the student swing her arm back to touch a target (pie plate) attached to the wall. The target is placed at the student's waist level in line with the throwing arm. The student then throws the ball. • With a partner standing behind the thrower, the thrower swings his arm back and tries to take an object out of the partner's hand. • Put paper on the wall. Have the student stand sideways with a marker in the throwing hand. As the student moves the throwing hand back, she draws a curvy line on the paper.
Student not stepping in opposition	• Tie a pinny or scarf around the leg opposite the throwing hand. • Use spots or footprints on the floor to indicate the correct foot placement. • Tape bubble wrap to the floor. Have the student step in opposition on that spot to create noise.
Releases ball too early or too late	• Suspend two ropes between game standards. The student must release the ball between the ropes. As he improves, remove one rope. • May use a partner's hand to indicate where the ball should be released.
Student not stepping toward target	• Use a line on the floor or put down tape. Challenge the student to step on the line when the ball is released. • Tape bubble wrap to the floor. Have the student step on the wrap to create noise. • Place two objects shoe-width apart in front of the student. These objects may be cones, domes, Styrofoam bricks, and so on. He must step so that his foot is placed between the two objects.
Body not in proper alignment on the follow-through	• Tell the student to point her belt buckle at the target on the follow-through. • Use a line on the floor or put down tape. Challenge the student to release the ball on the line and bring the throwing arm over the line as the ball is thrown.
Follow-through ends too high or too low	• Suspend two ropes between game standards. The student should touch the top rope on the follow-through. • May use a partner's hand to indicate where the follow-through should end.

Activities to Reinforce Underhand Throw

OVERHAND THROW

Ready Position

Facing target, feet shoulder-width apart, knees bent, eyes on target, object held in front of body in dominant hand.

T

Body turns as the feet pivot in place and nondominant side is toward the target. Bring the throwing arm back in a downward circular motion and extend the nonthrowing arm to create a T with the throwing hand extended away from the intended line of travel and the palm facing upward. The nonthrowing hand points toward the target.

Step and Throw

Step forward with the foot opposite the throwing arm, hips and shoulders rotate toward the target, front of the body faces the target, arm comes forward past the head.

Follow Through

Throwing hand continues toward the target and continues diagonally across the body.

Cue Sets

- Ready, T, step-throw-point, follow through
- Make a T, point and look, step and throw, squash the bug
- Turn to the T, step and throw, hug yourself
- Reach back, step, throw hard

Troubleshooting Chart

If you see	Then try this
Eyes not on target	• Have the student throw at a target he has designed. • Attach color targets to the wall. • Place a two-liter bottle upside down on top of a cone and have the student try to knock it off. • As an outside activity, have the student throw wet sponges at a target in an effort to soak the target with water. • Use aluminum pie plates for targets.
Not enough arm extension	• Encourage the student to use more force when throwing the object. (Students should be warmed up for all activities, especially this challenge.) • Have the student touch a wall located behind her while forming the T position and then throw the object. • With a partner standing behind the thrower, he will swing his arm back and try to take an object out of his partner's hand.
Hand of the throwing arm not going past the ear	• Ask the student to picture herself listening to music on a small radio and then throwing the radio past her ear to her partner. • Have the student use the Rocket Launcher activity in the step/throw/point station (see page 104 of CD-ROM). • Hang a yarn ball from a basketball goal so the ball is at ear height. Put the student in the T position (side orientation) and have her hit the ball with an open palm.
Student not stepping in opposition	• Tie a pinny or scarf around the foot opposite the throwing arm. • Use floor spots or footprints on the floor to indicate the proper foot placement. • Tape bubble wrap to the floor. Have the student step in opposition on that spot to create a noise.
Limited hip and shoulder rotation	• Have the student check the position of his belt buckle after the throw. The belt buckle should be pointing in the direction of the target. • Use rubber tubing or Dynabands. Have a partner stand behind the thrower. The partner holds the tubing to add resistance while the throwing student goes through the rotation motion.
Student not continuing the follow-through	• Place a tall cone in front of and to the nonthrowing side of the thrower's body. The cone should be far enough away so the student can step and extend the arm on the throw. The student throws the ball and then touches the top of the cone on the follow-through. • Have the students bow by crossing the arm across the body while bending forward.

Activities to Reinforce Overhand Throw

TWO-HAND OVERHEAD THROW

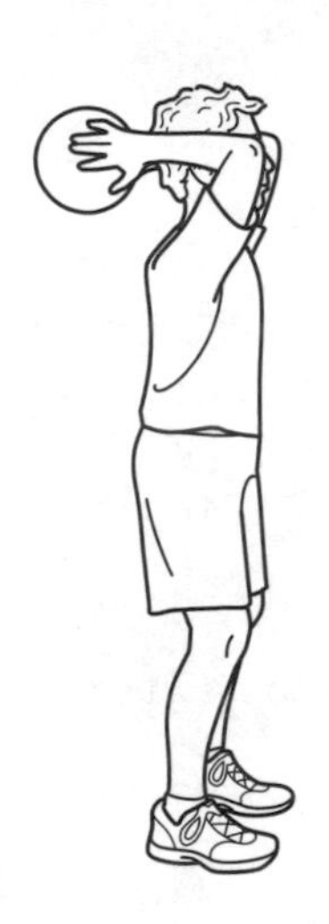

Ready Position

Facing target, feet shoulder-width apart, knees bent, eyes on target, hands held slightly behind and to the side of the ball. Ball is held at chest level.

Ball Behind Head

Ball is brought above and behind the head. The arms are bent.

Step and Throw

Step forward with one foot while extending arms and releasing ball toward target. There is a wrist snap with this action.

Follow Through

After the ball is released, hands are turned so that palms are facing away from each other and the thumbs are pointing downward.

Cue Sets

- Ready, ball over head, step and throw, follow through
- Ready, up, step and throw, follow through
- Ready, up, snap

Troubleshooting Chart

If you see	Then try this
Eyes not on the target	• Have the student throw to a target he has designed. • Place a two-liter bottle on top of a cone and have the student try to knock it off. • Use aluminum pie plates for targets.
Incorrect hand position on the ball	• Draw the hand positions on the ball. • Have the student put her hands in baby powder and then place them on a ball.
Student not stepping when throwing the ball	• Have the student step on a mat or a rug as she throws the ball. • Have the student stand near a line (a rope or tape on the floor can be used). She must step over the line while throwing the ball.
Arms not fully extended on the throw	• Have the student practice reaching out and grabbing an object placed an arm's length away from the body. • Place a suspended aluminum pie plate in front of the student and have him try to hit the pie plate with his outstretched hands.
Body not in proper alignment	• Tell the student to point her belt buckle at the target on the follow-through.
Ball hitting the target at too high or too low a level	• Suspend two ropes between two game standards. Place the ropes between waist high and neck high so that the ball can be thrown correctly through them and reach the target. • Have the student practice throwing the ball to a target on the wall. • The ball may be too heavy or too light for the student. Either give the student a more appropriately sized ball or move the child closer to (or farther away from) the target.

Activities to Reinforce Two-Hand Overhead Throw

CATCH ABOVE THE WAIST

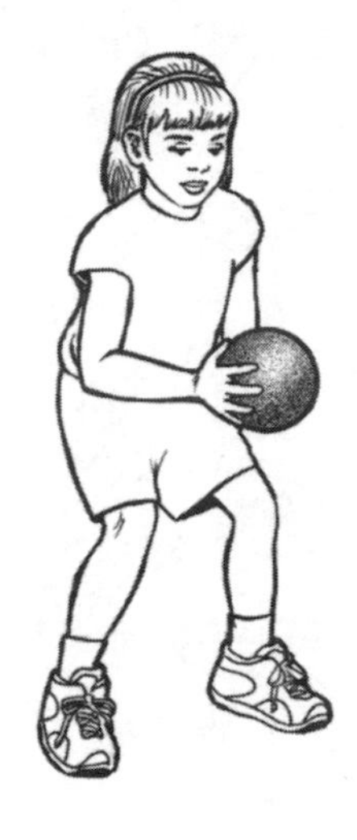

Ready Position

Facing the target, feet shoulder-width apart, knees bent, eyes on approaching object, elbows bent near sides, hands held in front of body. Thumbs are close to (or touching) one another and form the letter W.

Step and Reach

As the ball is released, step toward the thrower and extend the arms and hands to meet the ball. Hands are held in front of the body (elbows bent near sides) with thumbs together.

Fingers Only

Use only fingers and thumbs to catch the object. The ball should not be trapped against the body.

Give

Absorb the force of the object by bringing the arms back toward the body.

Cue Sets

- Reach out, catch, absorb the force
- Ready, reach, use your fingers, pull

Troubleshooting Chart

If you see	Then try this
Eyes not on the target	• Have the student's partner hold a ball while moving it through a variety of high levels and at various speeds. The student tracks the ball with her eyes. • The student hits a balloon up with her hands and tracks the movement of the balloon with her eyes.
Hands not in the catching position	• The throwing partner holds a ball and moves it to various high levels. The catching partner must move his hands in response to the ball position. (The ball is not thrown.) • The throwing partner tosses a balloon or beach ball at a variety of high levels. Watch for hand positions.
Body not in line with the oncoming object	• The partner tosses a balloon, beach ball, or Nerf ball into the air toward his partner. The receiving partner allows the object to hit his chest. Hands are out to the side—no catching. • The receiver moves in the direction the partner points.
Student not extending arms toward the ball	• Partners stand about arm's-length apart. The throwing partner extends her arms and holds the ball out. The receiving partner steps and extends her arms to take the ball. • Use a balloon or beach ball to provide more time for the receiver to reach out and catch the object.
Student not giving with the ball	• Elephant catch: As the receiving partner catches the ball, she pretends the ball is heavy like an elephant and absorbs the force. • Suspend a ball from the basketball goal. (A tetherball works well for this.) Students work with partners. Partners alternate pushing and catching the ball.
Student trapping the ball against the body	• Skunk ball: The student tosses the ball to his partner. If the ball hits the arms or chest as it is caught, the catcher has been sprayed by a skunk (stinker). Ask the class if there are any stinkers. • Detective: Have the student put baby powder on his hands before catching the ball. The receiving partner tries to catch the ball so he leaves only his fingerprints on the ball.
Student turns his head as ball approaches	• To build confidence, begin with a balloon, progress to a beach ball, and then to a soft textured ball. • Have the partner bounce the ball to him. With improvement, have the partner underhand toss the ball, and finally throw the ball overhand with light force.

Activities to Reinforce Catch Above the Waist

CATCH BELOW THE WAIST

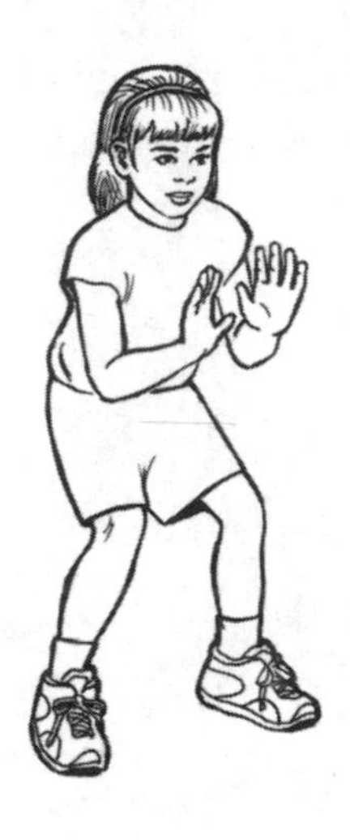

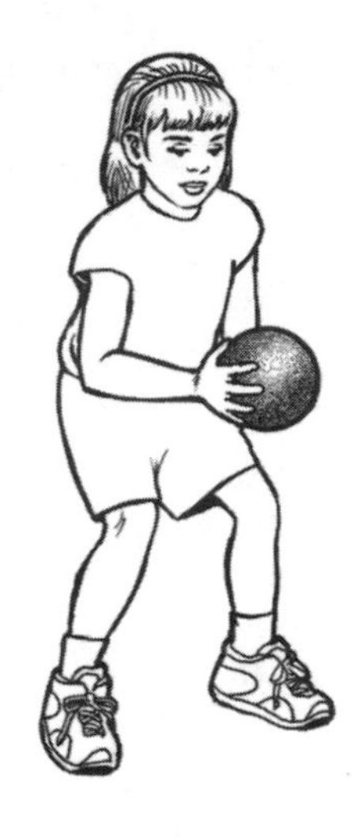

Ready Position

Facing the target, feet shoulder-width apart, knees bent, eyes on approaching object, elbows bent near sides, hands held in front of body.

Step and Reach

As the ball is released, step toward the thrower and extend the arms and hands to meet the ball. Hands are held in front of the body (elbows bent near sides) with little (pinkie) fingers together.

Fingers Only

Use only fingers and thumbs to catch the object. The ball should not be trapped against the body.

Give

Absorb the force of the object by bringing the arms back toward the body.

Cue Sets

- V, reach down, catch, absorb the force
- Ready, reach, grab, pull

Troubleshooting Chart

If you see	Then try this
Eyes not on the target	• Have the student's partner hold a ball while moving it through different levels below the waist and at different speeds. The student tracks the ball with her eyes. • The student hits a balloon up with her hands and tracks the movement of the balloon with her eyes.
Hands not in the catching position	• The throwing partner holds a ball and moves it to different levels below the waist. The catching partner must move his hands in response to the ball position. (The ball is not thrown.) • The throwing partner tosses the beach ball at a variety of low levels. Watch for hand positions.
Body not in line with the oncoming object	• The partner tosses a balloon, beach ball, or Nerf ball into the air toward his partner. The receiving partner allows the object to hit his chest. Hands are out to the side—no catching. • The receiver moves in the direction the partner points. The partner then adds the object.
Student not extending arms toward the ball	• Partners stand about arm's-length apart. The throwing partner extends her arms and holds the ball out. The receiving partner steps and extends her arms to take the ball. • Use a balloon or beach ball to provide more time for the receiver to reach out and catch the object.
Student not giving with the ball	• Elephant catch—As the receiving partner catches the ball, she pretends the ball is heavy like an elephant and absorbs the force. • Suspend a ball from the basketball goal at a low level. (A tetherball works well for this.) Students work with partners. Partners alternate pushing and catching the ball. • Water balloon toss (outside)—Have the student toss a water balloon to her partner and the partner tries to catch the balloon so it does not break. Stress the need to GIVE with the balloon.
Student trapping the ball against the body	• Skunk ball—The student tosses the ball to his partner. If the ball hits the arms, legs, or ground as it is caught, the catcher has been sprayed by a skunk (stinker). Ask the class if there are any stinkers. • Detective—Have the student put baby powder on his hands before catching the ball. The receiving partner tries to catch the ball so he leaves only his fingerprints on the ball.
Student turns his head as ball approaches	• To build confidence, begin with a balloon, progress to a beach ball, and then to a soft textured ball. • Have the partner bounce the ball to him. With improvement, have the partner underhand toss the ball and finally throw overhand with light force.

Activities to Reinforce Catch Below the Waist

BOUNCE PASS

Ready Position

Facing target, feet shoulder-width apart, knees bent, eyes on target, ball held with thumbs together and fingers on the sides of the ball. Hold the ball close to the body at chest level.

Step and Push

Step forward with one foot while extending arms FORWARD and DOWNWARD and releasing the ball so that it bounces closer to the target than to the passer.

Follow Through

After the ball is released, hands are turned so that palms are facing away from each other with the thumbs pointing downward. There is a wrist snap with this action.

Cue Sets

- Ready, step and push, follow through
- Ready, step and push, thumbs down
- Push, away

Troubleshooting Chart

If you see	Then try this
Eyes not on the target	• Have the student pass to a target he has designed. • Have students pass to different colored targets on the wall. • Place a two-liter bottle on top of a tall cone and have the student try to knock it off. • Place aluminum pie plates on the wall for targets.
Incorrect hand position on the ball	• Draw the hand positions on the ball. • Have the student put her hands in baby powder and then place them on a ball. • Balls are commercially available that have handprints already on them.
Student not stepping when passing the ball	• Have the student step on a mat or a rug as she passes the ball. • Have the student stand near a line (a rope or tape on the floor can be used). She must step over the line while passing the ball. • Tape bubble wrap to the floor. Have the student step on that spot to create a noise.
Arms not fully extended on the pass	• Have the student practice reaching out and grabbing an object placed at arm's length from the body. • Place a suspended aluminum pie plate in front of the student and have him try to hit the pie plate as he pushes his hands out for the bounce pass.
Body not in proper alignment on the follow-through	• Tell the student to point her belt buckle at the target on the follow-through. • Have a partner watch to make sure the chest is even with (or past) the stepping foot on the follow-through.
Ball not bouncing in the proper spot (hitting the ground too close or too far away from the target)	• Place two targets (pieces of tape or hula hoops) on the floor between the partners for them to hit. They should aim for the one closer to their partner. • Have the partners pass the ball under a rope (or volleyball net). • Place a dome between two partners. Have each partner try to hit the dome and push it past his partner.

Activities to Reinforce Bounce Pass

CHEST PASS

Ready Position

Facing target, feet shoulder-width apart, knees bent, eyes on target, ball held with thumbs together and fingers on the sides of the ball. Hold the ball close to the body at chest level.

Step and Push

Step forward with one foot while extending arms and releasing the ball toward the target.

Follow Through

After the ball is released, hands are turned so that palms are facing away from each other with the thumbs pointing downward. There is a wrist snap with this action.

Cue Sets

- Ready, step and push, follow through
- Ready, step and push, thumbs down
- Ready, away
- Push, away

Troubleshooting Chart

If you see	Then try this
Eyes not on the target	• Have the student pass to a target she has designed. • Have students pass to different colored targets on the wall. • Place a two-liter bottle on top of a tall cone and have the student try to knock it off. • Use aluminum pie plates for targets on the wall.
Incorrect hand position on the ball	• Draw the hand positions on the ball. • Have the student put her hands in baby powder and then place them on a ball. • Balls are commercially available that have handprints already on them.
Student not stepping when passing the ball	• Have the student step on a mat or a rug as she passes the ball. • Have the student stand near a line (rope or tape on the floor can be used). She must step over the line while passing the ball. • Tape bubble wrap to the floor. Have the student step on that spot to create a noise.
Arms not fully extended on the pass	• Have the student practice reaching out and grabbing an object placed an arm's length from the body. • Place a suspended aluminum pie plate in front of the student and have him try to hit the pie plate as he pushes his hands out for the chest pass.
Body not in proper alignment on the follow-through	• Tell the student to point her belt buckle at the target on the follow-through. • Have a partner watch to make sure the chest is equal to or past the stepping foot on the follow-through.
Ball hitting the target at a level too high or too low	• Suspend two ropes between two game standards. Place the ropes between waist and neck height so that the ball can be passed correctly through them and reach the target. • Have the student practice passing the ball to a target on the wall. • The ball may be too heavy or too light for the student. Either give the student a more appropriately sized ball or move the child closer to (or farther away from) the target.

Activities to Reinforce Chest Pass

BASKETBALL DRIBBLE

Ready Position

Knees bent, feet shoulder-width apart, eyes looking forward, ball held in both hands in front of the body.

Push

One hand contacts the ball at waist level or below and pushes it downward using the finger pads only. (Make sure students are using the pads of all four fingers and the thumb. If they are told to use their fingertips to dribble, the fingertips become so rigid at ball contact that the children are unable to develop a feel for the ball.) The wrist flexes and the elbow extends downward as the ball is pushed down.

Eyes Forward

As the ball is contacted, the head is up and the eyes are focused forward.

Keep Ball in Front of Body

The ball should be bounced diagonally in front of the body and away from the feet.

Cue Sets

- Ready, wave goodbye, hello
- Use your tickle fingers, push

Troubleshooting Chart

If you see	Then try this
Ball bouncing lower and lower	• Review the concept of force with the student. • Hold the ball on the bottom while the student pushes on the top of the ball. You give with the ball and then push it back up. It is a continuous movement. • Have the student work with a partner. The student pushes the partner's hand down while the partner offers light resistance.
Student using part of the hand besides the fingers	• Have the student practice "spider push-ups" (finger pads of each hand push against each other so the palms of each hand come close to one another and then move away). Finger pads stay in contact at all times. Perform this several times. • Hold the ball on the bottom while the student pushes with the finger pads on the top of the ball. You give with the ball and then push it back up while watching the student's finger pads. This is a continuous movement.
Student keeping the wrist straight or locked	• Have the student practice waving goodbye to the floor. • Hold the ball on the bottom while the student pushes on the top of the ball. You control the movement of the ball while watching the student's wrist. • Place a piece of paper on a wall extending from knee to chest level. Have the student face the paper with a marker in her hand. The student marks the paper using an up-and-down movement of the wrist.
Arm not fully extended while pushing the ball down	• Have the student practice the arm motion without the ball. • Place a piece of paper on a wall extending from knee to chest level. Have the student face the paper with a marker in her hand. The student marks the paper using an up-and-down movement of the wrist and arm.
Student watching the ball instead of looking forward	• The student places one hand above his mouth and parallel to the ground. This will block his view of the ball. • Have the student dribble a ball while you hold up a picture or a number of fingers for a couple of seconds. The student must be able to tell you what he saw. • Place a softball glove (or deflated playground ball) on the student's head. He must dribble without letting the glove (ball) fall off.
Ball bouncing off the student's feet	• Have the student stand on a specific spot on the floor. Place a poly spot or piece of tape next to the student and have the student dribble the ball on the spot. • Put a hula hoop on the floor and have the student dribble the ball inside the hoop. (Or the student may stand in the hoop and dribble the ball outside of the hoop.) • Have the student try to dribble while on both knees. Once this is accomplished, have the student kneel on one knee and dribble.
Student is unable to control the ball when moving	• Allow the student to dribble only three times in a row while moving and then stop. As he becomes more proficient, increase the number of dribbles allowed. • Play music as the student dribbles. When the music stops, the student must freeze and maintain control of the ball while dribbling in place. Students unable to maintain control must decrease their speed.

Activities to Reinforce Basketball Dribble

SOCCER DRIBBLE

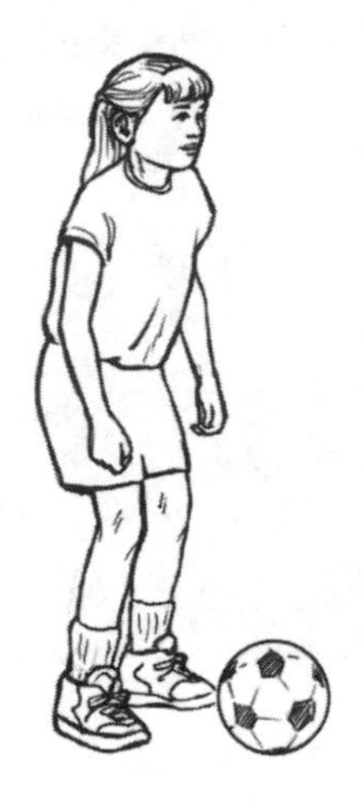

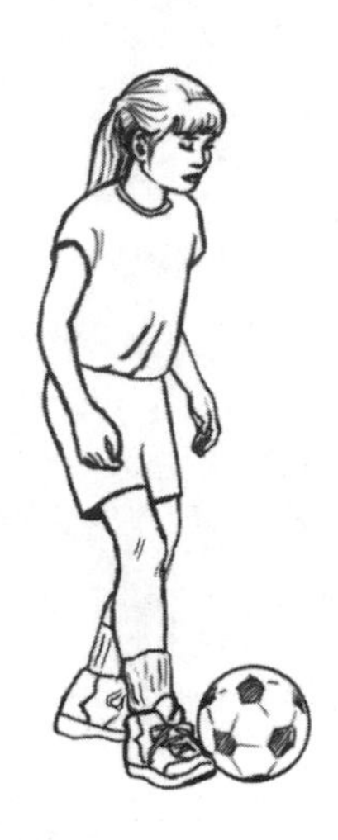

Ready Position

Ball on ground directly below head, feet shoulder-width apart, knees bent.

Foot Taps Ball

Perform a short series of taps with the inside or outside of the foot (not the toe). Use of the nondominant foot should be practiced and encouraged.

Keep Ball Close

The ball should be on the ground directly below the head as it is contacted; eyes look forward. Keep the ball within two to four feet while dribbling.

Move With Ball

The soccer dribble is a movement activity and should be performed at a speed faster than a walk.

Albemarle County Physical Education Curriculum Revision Committee, 1996, 5-6.

Cue Sets

- Eyes up, tap, go
- Use the flat part of your foot, easy taps, keep it close

Troubleshooting Chart

If you see	Then try this
Student using the toe to dribble the ball	• Suspend a two-liter soda bottle from a net or rope between two game standards. The bottle should be suspended so that it is no more than one inch off the ground. The student must tap the bottle from side to side using the inside or outside of the foot. • Students work in pairs. One partner dribbles the ball a specified distance. The other partner counts the number of times the toe touches the ball. The object is to obtain a score of zero.
Student not using short taps to dribble the ball	• Review the concept of force. • Give each student a ball to dribble. Walk through the playing area and try to take the ball away from any student who taps it too far away. The object is for the students to keep all balls away from you. • Set up cones approximately two to four feet apart and scattered throughout the playing area. The student must dribble the ball through the cones and tap the ball at least once before passing any cone.
Student always using the same foot	• Have students work in pairs. One partner dribbles the ball a specified distance. The student dribbling must alternate feet during the dribble. The other partner counts every time the feet do not alternate. The object is to obtain a score of zero. • Suspend a two-liter soda bottle from a net or rope between two game standards. The bottle should be suspended so that it is no more than one inch off the ground. The student must tap the bottle from side to side using the inside or outside of the foot.
Student watching the ball instead of looking forward	• Students work in pairs. Using an empty milk jug, deflated ball, or Nerf ball, one student tries to move the object through the playing area while maintaining eye contact with her partner. • Have the student work with a partner, playing keep-away. • Have the student dribble a ball while you hold up a picture or a number of fingers for a couple of seconds. The student must be able to tell you what he saw. • Have the students work in pairs. One partner dribbles a ball while following the movements of the other partner. The leading partner should begin with a walk and then increase the speed as the dribbler becomes more proficient.
Student walking while dribbling the ball	• Students work in pairs. One partner is a tagger. The tagger may walk fast to try to catch the dribbler and get the ball. The dribbler may walk fast or run to stay away from the tagger. The object is to keep the ball away from the tagger. • Use several taggers.

Activities to Reinforce Soccer Dribble

UNDERHAND STRIKE

Ready Position

Face the direction of the strike, feet shoulder-width apart, eyes looking at ball, ball held in nondominant hand in front of the body at waist level.

Step and Swing

Pull striking arm back to at least waist level, lean forward, step forward with opposite foot while dominant hand strikes the ball in front of the body at waist level or below.

Hit

Strike the underside of the ball with the heel of the hand while continuing the step with the foot opposite the striking hand.

Follow Through

Hand continues in the direction of the ball but does not go beyond the height of the shoulder.

Cue Sets

- Ready, step, hit
- Hold it low, step, hit
- Start, extend, step and swing, follow through
- Ready, arm back, step and hit, follow through

Troubleshooting Chart

If you see	Then try this
Ball not held in front of body	• Place a mirror in front of the student so he can see his arm and hand placement. • The student works with a partner. The student gets into the correct position, and the partner places the ball into his hand.
Arm not going back far enough	• Hang a balloon from a net or rope suspended between two game standards. Have the student stand in front of the balloon and swing her arm back until it hits the balloon. This can also be done with the student standing with her back to the wall and swinging her arm back to touch the wall. • Place a large piece of paper on the wall. Have the student stand sideways to the paper and mark his waist height. Swing the student's arm back and draw the arc of the backswing on the paper for him to see.
Student not stepping or stepping forward on the wrong foot	• Tie a pinny or scarf on the opposite leg. • Place a spot or footprint in front of the student. He must step onto the spot or footprint before hitting the ball. • Tape bubble wrap to the floor. Have the student step in opposition on that spot to create a noise.
Student throwing the ball up in the air before striking	• Have a partner touch the arm holding the ball. The partner needs to apply enough resistance so the student can feel the arm remaining stationary. • Hang a balloon from a net or rope suspended between two game standards. Have the student hold the balloon and strike it. If the student tosses the balloon, he will see a bend in the balloon rope.
Student not using the heel of the hand to strike the ball	• Hang a damp sponge from a volleyball net or rope suspended between two game standards. Have the student hit the sponge with the heel of her hand. Check to see where the water is on the hand. • Partners face each other; one has her hand outstretched with the palm down. Using light force and an underhand motion, the other partner swings her arm and strikes the first partner's outstretched hand with the heel of her hand.
Swing arm not following through	• Suspend a net or rope between two game standards so the bottom of the net is at the student's shoulder height. Have the student perform the skill without a ball, continuing the arm swing until the heel of the hand touches the net. • Partners face each other; one has his hand outstretched with the palm down at shoulder height. Using light force and an underhand motion, the other partner swings his arm and strikes the first partner's outstretched hand with the heel of his hand.

Activities to Reinforce Underhand Strike

SIDE-ARM STRIKE

Ready Position

Front of the body toward the target, eyes on the target, feet shoulder-width apart, knees bent, hands parallel with palms facing each other and fingers pointing forward.

T

Body turns as the feet pivot in place, side to target, arms extended in the shape of a T. Extend the striking hand away from the intended line of travel with the palm facing outward. Hold the ball toward the target in the nonstriking hand. Drop the ball. Eyes are on the ball throughout the movement.

Step and Hit

Step toward the target with the foot opposite the striking arm. Arm swings through as the hips and shoulders rotate toward the target, allowing the front body surface to face the target.

Follow Through

Hand continues in the direction of the strike.

Cue Sets

- Ready, T, step, follow through
- Start, go, hit
- Drop, go, whack it
- Start, step and hit

Troubleshooting Chart

If you see	Then try this
Student not keeping eyes on ball	• Place a two-liter bottle upside down on top of a cone and have the student try to knock it off. • Draw a picture on the ball and have the student focus on this as he watches the ball. If the ball has words on it, just use the words. • The student's partner bounces a ball to him using light force. He must move so the ball will touch his belt buckle.
Student not turning side to the target	• Draw two arrows perpendicular to each other in front of both of the student's feet as she is standing in the ready position. Have the student practice rotating on the balls of her feet to turn her side to the target. • Have the student's partner give a verbal cue to turn as the ball comes toward the student. • Have the student's partner bounce a ball to her. The student must rotate so the ball will touch the side of her body.
Student not pulling the striking arm back	• Have the student turn and use the striking arm to touch a wall located behind him. • The student's partner stands behind him with one hand held in the police officer "stop" position. The student turns and pulls his arm back until it touches the palm of the partner's hand.
Student not taking a step forward	• Use spots or footprints on the floor to indicate to the student where the opposite foot should be placed during the strike. • Have the student step over a line or flat object with the opposite foot before striking. • Use a small, nonskid "bug" (floor spot) in front of the stepping foot and ask the student to step on the bug as she strikes the ball. • Tie a pinny or scarf around the opposite leg. • Tape bubble wrap to the floor. Have the student step in opposition on that spot to create a noise.
Limited hip and shoulder rotation	• Have the student check his belt buckle position after the strike. It should be facing in the direction of the target. • Have a partner hold rubber tubing or Dynabands to add resistance while the student goes through the rotation motion.
Striking arm not coming through in an extended position	• Hang an object (e.g., small wind chime, sheet, pie plate) from a net or rope suspended between two game standards. Have the student touch the object as the striking arm moves forward. • Have the student's partner hold an object (hula hoop, bean bag, plastic bottle). The student takes the object out of the partner's hand as the student moves her arm forward.
Student not continuing the follow-through	• Suspend a balloon from a basketball goal. Have the student perform the striking skill and touch the balloon with her hand as she finishes.

Activities to Reinforce Side-Arm Strike

TWO-HAND SIDE-ARM STRIKE

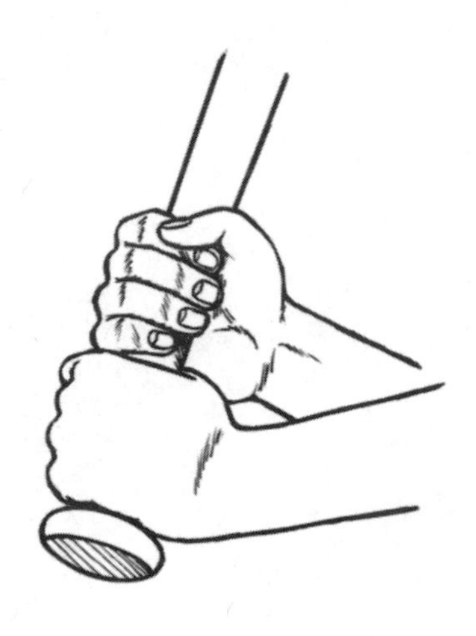

Ready Position

- Nondominant side toward the intended target, chin placed over the nondominant shoulder, hands gripping the bat are level with the armpit with the dominant hand above the nondominant hand, bat is held behind the dominant shoulder, and dominant elbow is parallel to the ground.
- To find proper foot placement, the student's front foot is in line with the tee. The student then extends her arms so that the bat touches the tee. The student then takes one step back from the intended direction of the strike.

Step and Swing

Step forward with opposite foot while back foot remains stationary. Weight transfers from the back foot to the front foot as the hips and shoulders begin to rotate.

Hit

Arms extend and ball is contacted in front of the body and in line with the front foot. Use the upper half of the bat when striking the ball.

Follow Through

Bat continues past the point of the strike, back shoulder moves to position under the chin, and both hands remain on the bat.

Albemarle County Physical Education Curriculum Revision Committee, 1996, 3-1.

Cue Sets

- Ready, step and swing, hit, follow through
- Ready, step, swing
- Bat back, step and hit, shoulder
- Ready, swing through the ball

Troubleshooting Chart

If you see	Then try this
Back elbow not parallel to ground	• Have the student demonstrate the ready position (without bat) with the teacher or partner lifting the elbow to the correct position, if needed. • Set up a mirror and have the student demonstrate the ready position.
Feet not in proper position in relation to the tee (or plate)	• Place tape on the floor and have the student stand on the tape. • Place a jump rope on the ground perpendicular to the plate. The student must stand behind the rope before hitting the ball.
Student not stepping forward on opposite foot	• Place a footprint or spot where the student should step. • Have the student practice the swing a set number of times while the partner counts the number of times the student does not step. The object is to get a score of zero. • Tie a pinny or scarf around the opposite leg. • Tape bubble wrap to the floor. Have the student step in opposition on that spot to create a noise.
Limited hip and shoulder rotation	• Have the student check the position of his belt buckle. After the student hits the ball, the belt buckle should be pointing in the direction of the target. • Without a bat, use rubber tubing or Dynabands. Have a partner hold the tubing. This will add resistance while the student goes through the rotation motion.
Arms not coming through in an extended position	• Hang an object (small wind chime, sheet, pie plates) from a net or rope suspended between two game standards. Have the student touch the object as the arms swing forward. • Have the student's partner hold an object (hula hoop, bean bag, plastic bottle). The student takes the object out of the partner's hand as the student swings his arms forward.
Head moving during the swing or student not keeping eyes on ball	• Place a baseball or softball glove (or deflated playground ball) on the student's head. The student swings the bat. The goal is for the student to keep the head stationary, which will keep the glove (ball) on her head. • Color half of a six-inch ball one color and the other half remains its original color (you can use a marker, paint, or chalk). After hitting a pitched or tossed ball, the student must be able to tell the teacher or a partner what color he hit.
Student not continuing the follow-through	• Have the student practice swinging an imaginary bat. The student should focus on keeping the head still and rotating the shoulders so that the rotation progresses from the front shoulder under the chin to the back shoulder under the chin.

Activities to Reinforce Two-Hand Side-Arm Strike

Individual:

- Batting Tee Challenges . . 252
- Whack It 253

Partner:

- Challenges 253
- Moving Target 253

Group:

- Create Your Own Activity . 254

KICK

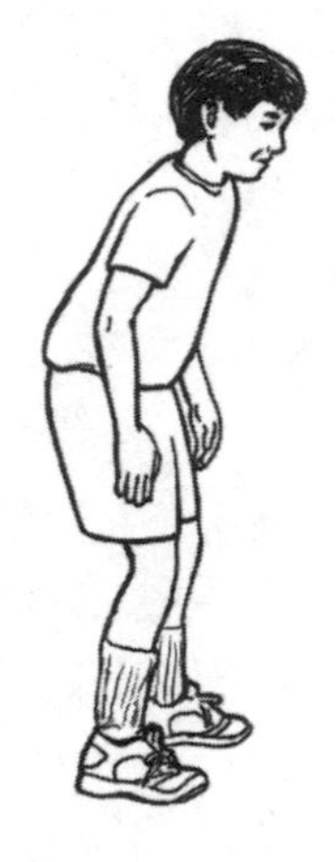

Ready Position

Stand behind the ball; focus eyes on the ball.

Step and Leap

Step forward on the kicking foot to generate power for the kick. Leap forward on the nonkicking foot and place the toes beside the ball. Lean forward with the kicking foot off the ground.

Kick

Contact the ball at or slightly below the center with either the laces of the shoe or the inside of the foot.

Follow Through

Arm opposite the kicking leg swings forward, and kicking foot continues forward in the direction of the kick. There is a backward lean on the follow-through.

From Albemarle County Physical Education Curriculum Revision Committee, 1996, 5-1.

Cue Sets

- Ready, step, leap, kick, follow through
- Approach, leap, plant, kick, follow through
- Ready, leap, kick, high
- Ready, and . . . kick

Troubleshooting Chart

If you see	Then try this
Eyes not looking at the ball	• Have the student draw a face on the ball or use any words already on the ball for a focal point. • Place three types of balls in front of the student (e.g., playground, Nerf, and soccer). Call out the ball the student is supposed to approach and touch (not kick).
Student not stepping forward on the kicking foot or not taking a large enough step	• Place an object (e.g., footprint, color spot) in front of the student for her to step on. • Place an object (jump rope) in front of the student for her to step over. • Tie a pinny or scarf around the opposite leg. • Tape bubble wrap to the floor. Have the student step in opposition on that spot to create a noise.
Student stepping onto the nonkicking foot instead of leaping	• Have the student practice the leap before she tries to use it with the kick. • Place two ropes parallel to each other on the ground for the student to leap over.
No forward lean	• Have the student check his shadow for the forward lean. • Have the student pretend to be a runner leaning forward to win a race. Once the student can lean forward, have him practice leaping and leaning.
Toes of the nonkicking foot not placed beside or diagonal to the ball	• Place a nonskid footprint next to the ball and have the student practice the leap and land on the footprint. • Have the student's partner check to see if part of the foot is hidden by the ball.
Knee of the kicking leg straight as it swings behind the body or the kicking leg not off the ground behind the body	• Place a six-inch cone so that the student must leap and the knee of the kicking leg travels over the top of the cone. No part of the student's foot or leg should touch the cone. • Have the student watch her shadow to check the position of the kicking leg. • Have the student's partner check the position of the kicking leg.
Shoelaces (or instep) of the kicking foot not contacting the ball below the center of the ball	• Draw a line on the ball and challenge the student to kick the ball below the line. • Place baby powder or chalk below the center of the ball. Have the student kick the ball and then check the ball and the foot to see where contact was made. • Set up two six-inch cones with a strip of tape or string across the top of the cones. Have the student place the ball on the side opposite him. He should try to kick the ball while keeping the foot below the tape or string.
Arm opposite the kicking leg not swinging forward or the kicking foot not continuing in the direction of the ball	• Have the student stand and practice swinging the kicking leg forward to touch the fingers of the outstretched opposite hand. • Set up a rope at waist level to the student and have him practice the kick without a ball. He must follow through on the kick so that the kicking foot and the opposite arm touch the bottom of the rope.

Activities to Reinforce the Kick

PUNT

Ready Position

Stand in a stride position with the nonpunting foot slightly in front of the punting foot, feet shoulder-width apart. Distribute weight equally on both feet, bend knees, hold ball with both hands in front of the body at waist level.

Leap

Leap onto the nonpunting foot in the direction of the punt, lifting the punting foot off the ground behind the body.

Drop and Punt

Drop the ball from outstretched hands. Bring the punting leg forward and contact the ball on top of the punting foot (shoelaces). There is a backward lean at contact and the leg and foot should be at full extension.

Follow Through

Leg continues in the direction of the punt as the opposite arm comes forward for balance. There is a backward lean at contact.

Cue Sets

- Ready, leap, drop and punt, follow through
- Ready, drop, punt
- Ready, drop, pow

Troubleshooting Chart

If you see	Then try this
Arms not extended	• Have the punting student take a step forward, extend the ball out, and give it to her partner. The partner takes the ball. • Have the student watch her shadow to check for arm extension.
Student not stepping forward on the punting foot or taking too short a step	• Place an object (e.g., footprint, color spot) in front of the student to step on. • Place an object (jump rope) in front of the student for him to step over. • Tie a pinny or scarf around the nondominant leg. • Tape bubble wrap to the floor. Have the student step in opposition on that spot to create a noise.
Student stepping onto the nonpunting foot instead of leaping	• Have the student practice the leap before he tries to use it with the punt. • Place two ropes parallel to each other on the ground for the student to leap over.
No forward lean before contact	• Have the student watch her shadow to check for the forward lean.
Knee of the punting leg remains straight as it swings behind the body or the punting leg not off the ground behind the body	• Place a six-inch cone so that the student must leap and the knee of the punting leg travels over the top of the cone. No part of the student's foot or leg should touch the cone. • Have the student watch his shadow to check the position of the punting leg. • Have the student's partner check the position of the student's punting leg.
Student tossing the ball into the air	• Have the student stand and practice dropping the ball. • Have the student step, leap, and then drop the ball into a box or a hula hoop. • Have the student's partner watch to see if the ball is dropped or tossed.
Top of the punting foot (shoelaces) not contacting the ball	• Place baby powder or chalk on the ball. Have the student punt the ball and then check the ball and foot to see what part of the foot contacted which part of the ball. • Suspend a beanbag or Nerf ball from a rope strung between two game standards. Have the student practice touching the top of her foot to the suspended object.
Arm opposite the punting leg not swinging forward or the punting foot not continuing in the direction of the ball	• Have the student stand and practice swinging her punting leg forward to touch the fingers of the outstretched opposite hand. • Set up a rope at waist level to the student and have her practice the punt without a ball. She must follow through on the punt so that the punting foot and the opposite arm touch the bottom of the rope.

Activities to Reinforce the Punt

VOLLEYBALL FOREARM PASS

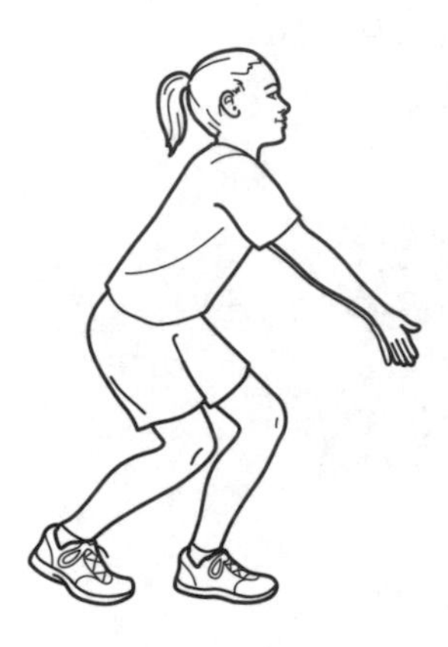

Ready Position

Eyes on ball, knees bent, feet shoulder-width apart, one foot in front of the other, hands together, and arms parallel to thighs.

Move to the Ball

Move so that the arms are below the ball.

Hit and Extend

Wait until ball is at a medium to low level. Ball contacts lower half of forearm. When the ball contacts the arm, it is below shoulder level. Legs extend as ball is contacted to generate power.

Follow Through

Hands remain joined and arms do not go past shoulder level.

Cue Sets

- Ready, move to ball, hit and lift, follow through
- Ready, move, lift
- Ready, move, bump
- Get under the ball

Troubleshooting Chart

If you see	Then try this
Incorrect hand position	• Teach the fist method: Have the student make a fist with one hand with thumb on top. Take the other hand and wrap it around the fist with thumb on top. The two thumbs are together. Extend arms downward to create a flat surface for contact. • Place a piece of tape diagonally across the palm of the bottom hand and have the student place his other hand on top of it. Once the hands curl, the little-finger side of the top hand will be along the tape line.
Arms not extended and parallel, elbows are bent	• A partner stands beside the student. The student assumes correct hand position and places his hands in his partner's hands. The teacher tosses the ball for the student to forearm pass. • Suspend a beach ball from a basketball goal so the ball is waist level to the student. Have the student extend his arms and try to pass the ball while keeping his arms straight.
Arms swing up past shoulder level	• Place a piece of paper on the wall in front of the student and draw a line parallel to the floor slightly below the student's shoulder level. Have the student hold a marker in his outstretched hands and draw a line up the paper to the parallel line. • Suspend a rope between two game standards slightly lower than the student's shoulders. Toss the ball to the student who will hit the ball and stop his arm swing when he touches the rope.
Feet are not in a stride position	• Place two tape marks on the floor for the student to place his feet. • Have the student walk around. When you say, "Now," he assumes a stride position with his feet in the proper position for the forearm pass.
Student does not lift with his legs during the forearm pass	• Student assumes a stride position with his knees bent and arms in the proper position. On your signal, he extends his legs and lifts his arms slightly. • Suspend a rope between two game standards slightly higher than the student's head. As he hits the ball, he must extend his legs and touch the rope with the top of his head.
Student does not get under the ball	• Student holds his arms in the proper position and moves to catch a tossed ball on his outstretched arms. • Student places baby powder on his forearms. He moves under the ball and tries to hit the ball so powder sticks to the ball.

Activities to Reinforce Volleyball Forearm Pass

VOLLEYBALL OVERHEAD PASS

Ready Position

Feet shoulder-width apart, knees bent, and head back. Hands in front of forehead with index fingers and thumbs forming a window. Look through the window for the ball.

Move to the Ball

Move to the ball so that the head is under the ball.

Extend to Hit

Contact the lower back of the ball with fingers and thumbs. Extend arms and legs for force. Wrists snap at contact.

Follow Through

Palms are facing away from each other, thumbs are pointing toward target, and arms and legs are extended.

Cue Sets

- Ready, move to the ball, extend to hit, follow through
- Get under the ball, use your view finder, extend, push hands away
- Bend and extend
- Get under the ball

Troubleshooting Chart

If you see	Then try this
Student is not forming a window with fingers or the window is not held above the head	• Play a game of I Spy, where the student must look up through a window formed with the fingers and thumbs to find the object mentioned. These items may be permanent overhead fixtures in the gymnasium: basketball baskets, specific ceiling tiles.
Student is not moving under the ball	• Shine a flashlight on the ceiling and have the student move to get under the light. • Toss a ball to the student, who must get under the ball and catch it directly over her head.
Student loses her balance after performing the overhead pass	• Using two poly spots or a tape line on the floor, have the student place a foot on each spot or stand just behind the line. She should pass the ball to a partner. Neither student should move off the spots or over the line on the follow-through.
Student hits the ball with the palm instead of the fingers	• Put the ball on her fingers as she looks through the "window." • Toss the ball to the student and have her try to hit the ball without making a sound.
Student pushes the ball down instead of hitting it up and out	• Have the student pass the ball and then look at her finger and hand position. • Have the student try to make the ball go through the basketball hoop using the overhead pass.
Student does not extend her arms and legs when striking the ball	• Have the student practice going from the ready position to the extend to hit position without the ball. • Have the student try to pass the ball close to, but not touching, the ceiling.

Activities to Reinforce Volleyball Overhead Pass

ABOUT THE AUTHORS

Vonnie Colvin, EdD, is an associate professor in Longwood University's department of health, recreation and kinesiology. In addition to her teaching duties, she works with student teachers in the schools and is the program coordinator for the physical and health education teacher education program in her department. Before coming to Longwood University in 2004, Colvin was a member of the department of kinesiology and health promotion at the University of Kentucky for nine years. During her tenure in Kentucky, she received the Outstanding University Physical Educator Award and an Outstanding Service Award from the Kentucky Association for Health, Physical Education, Recreation and Dance in 2002.

Colvin is a member of both the American Alliance for Health, Physical Education, Recreation and Dance (AAHPERD) and the Virginia Association for Health, Physical Education, Recreation and Dance. She served as vice president of physical education for the Kentucky state organization in 1999. In addition, Colvin served on the *Strategies* editorial board from 1999 to 2002.

Before moving to higher education in 1995, Colvin taught physical education in Louisa County, Virginia, for 21 years—8 years at the elementary level, 2 at the middle school level, and 11 at the high school level. During that time she also worked with student teachers from Norfolk State University and Virginia Tech.

Colvin lives in Farmville, Virginia, and enjoys hiking, gardening, and reading.

Nancy Markos, MEd, CAPE, is the 2002 National Elementary Physical Education Teacher of the Year for the National Association for Sport and Physical Education (NASPE) and the 2003 Outstanding Elementary School Teacher for the Curry School of Education at the University of Virginia. Markos has been an elementary physical education and health specialist in Albemarle County school system in Charlottesville, Virginia, since 1984. She has been a clinical instructor for the University of Virginia since 1985, where she mentors students in the physical education and adapted physical education programs. Before coming to Virginia, Markos taught physical education at the elementary level for three years in Maryland and at the middle school level for five years in Maryland and Rhode Island.

Markos is a member of the National Education Association; AAHPERD; Virginia Association of Health, Physical Education, Recreation and Dance; the education sorority Delta Kappa Gamma; and the professional education fraternity Phi Delta Kappa. She is past president of the Albemarle

Education Association. Markos was a member of the writing and revision teams for the Standards of Learning for Physical Education and for the *Physical Education Resource Guide* for the Virginia Department of Education. She received two grants, one from Dominion Virginia Power and the other from Albemarle County. The Dominion grant is for promoting kinesthetic learning for all students and the Albemarle grant is for promoting the use of personal digital assistants in the gym.

Markos lives in Earlysville, Virginia, and enjoys spending time with her family as well as running, mountain biking, and playing racquetball and golf.

Pam Walker, MEd, has been an elementary physical education and health specialist in the Albemarle County school system in Charlottesville, Virginia, for 29 years. She has spent the last 24 years at Red Hill Elementary in North Garden, Virginia. Walker has been a clinical instructor at the University of Virginia, where she works with practicum students and student teachers. Currently she works with student teachers from Longwood University. Walker was named the 1995 Elementary Physical Education Teacher of the Year by the Virginia Association of Health, Physical Education, Recreation and Dance.

In addition to her membership in the state association, Walker is a member of AAHPERD, the National Education Association, the education sorority Delta Kappa Gamma, and the professional education fraternity Phi Delta Kappa.

In 1997, along with coauthor Nancy Markos, Walker cofounded Physical Education for All Kids (PEAK), an organization committed to educating parents, teachers, and administrators on the importance of providing effective daily physical education to all students.

Walker lives in Schuyler, Virginia, and enjoys swimming, golfing, and camping.

CD-ROM USER INSTRUCTIONS

System Requirements

You can use this CD-ROM on either a Windows®-based PC or a Macintosh computer.

Windows

- IBM PC compatible with Pentium® processor
- Windows® 98/2000/XP
- Adobe Reader® 8.0
- 4x CD-ROM drive

Macintosh

- Power Mac® recommended
- System 10.4 or higher
- Adobe Reader®
- 4x CD-ROM drive

User Instructions

Windows

1. Insert the *Teaching the Nuts and Bolts of Physical Education CD-ROM*. (Note: The CD-ROM must be present in the drive at all times.)
2. Select the "My Computer" icon from the desktop.
3. Select the CD-ROM drive.
4. Open the "Start.pdf" file. See the "Start.pdf" file for a description of the CD-ROM contents.

Macintosh

1. Insert the Teaching the Nuts and Bolts of Physical Education CD-ROM. (Note: The CD-ROM must be present in the drive at all times.)
2. Double-click the CD icon located on the desktop.
3. Open the "Start.pdf" file. See the "Start.pdf" file for a description of the CD-ROM contents.

For customer support, contact Technical Support:

Phone: 217-351-5076 Monday through Friday (excluding holidays) between 7:00 a.m. and 7:00 p.m. (CST).

Fax: 217-351-2674

E-mail: support@hkusa.com